WHAT SHOULD WE REALLY PRAY FOR?

A Catholic Guide to Prayer of Petition

TRACY O'SULLIVAN, O.CARM.

twentythirdpublications.com

Twenty-Third Publications
One Montauk Avenue, Suite 200
New London, CT 06320
(860) 437-3012 or (800) 321-0411
www.twentythirdpublications.com

Copyright © 2020 Tracy O'Sullivan. All rights reserved.

No part of this publication may be reproduced in any manner without prior written permission of the publisher. Write to the Permissions Editor.

Cover photo: ©Shutterstock.com / NATNN

ISBN: 978-1-62785-546-4
Printed in the U.S.A.

A division of Bayard, Inc.

INTRODUCTION

"Our Thoughts and Prayers"

A Serious Commitment

We often tell people that we will pray for them or that they will be in our thoughts and prayers. This can mean several different things. When we are truly sincere, it almost always means we have come to a sense of our helplessness and mortality. We are turning to God for assistance. At the other end of the spectrum, this is a polite way to exit a scene when our concern is minimal. In between, there are various degrees of discomfort that reflect our true feelings.

When we make a commitment to pray for someone or some cause or issue, we are taking on a serious responsibility. We seldom think about it in those terms.

What exactly are we doing when we are engaging in the prayer of petition? Are we trying to give an all-knowing God a 9-1-1 call? Of course, God is aware of the specific situation with an infinitely deeper clarity and depth than we could ever have. Are we trying to get God to raise the intensity of divine love and compassion? God's love for every human being is already without limits. There is no thermostat on God's love that allows us to turn up the intensity. Are we trying to change God's mind to be more open to our point of view? That, of course, puts us in charge. God is seen as a butler waiting for our summons. This caricature of prayer is too often the common practice. Then there are the times where our continual pleading seems to be based on a strong hope that we will wear God down with our persistence. Our strong resolution in prayer needs to be based on God's faithfulness and mercy.

I

Exploring Prayer of Petition

I would like to share a personal story as an example of the teachings on prayer.

From my earliest moment of consciousness prayer was part of my life. My Irish immigrant mother filled the house with phrases like "Sweet Jesus," "Holy Mother of God," "Jesus, Mary, and Joseph," and the like. Mass on Sunday was as normal as breakfast in the morning. The same prayerful atmosphere permeated my school, St. Laurence, on the South Side of Chicago.

Then, in fourth grade, I came to the first of many crises

with prayer. I was beginning a journey of growth that continues to this day. Prayer may appear simple and beautiful. Over time I came to learn that it is also complex and demanding.

It was 1944 in the fall. Our fourth-grade teacher, Sister Julia Anne, had us pray three Hail Marys each day of that week for Notre Dame to defeat Army on Saturday. Since we believed God was Catholic, we supposed that this great Catholic university was also God's favorite team. When they lost 59-0 I had a serious problem. What kind of God would let our prayer for his team go unanswered, and at 59-0? That was just too much for my fourth-grade mind and heart to handle. It was going to take a great deal of life's journey for me to learn that I had the problem and not God.

Slowly, I got over the immediate crisis. However, the seeds of doubt and confusion were planted. Nevertheless, I continued to pray but with a little more wariness about an easy fix from on high.

Eight years later I had a more mature experience of the complexity of prayer. My passion in life was football. I was quarterback and co-captain on the Mt. Carmel team. My prayer was to beat St. Leo, the great obstacle to a fourth consecutive city championship. Each day for more than six months, I prayed three Hail Marys for victory over the Leo Lions.

On the day of the game in early November, not only did we win, but I threw the winning TD pass in the final minutes.

However, there was a small problem in my heavenly scenario. Earlier we had lost to De LaSalle, the only loss to this school in what was to turn out to be a forty-year span. This meant we had to play St. Leo again to break the tie and go on to the championship game. In the playoff game against Leo, we lost in the last minute.

I went into a deep desolation for several months. In the eighth grade I had thought about the seminary. This was quickly buried in my heart by my dreams of glory in football. Then one day walking home from school, in this period of darkness, God gave me the real answer to my prayers. The idea of the seminary was not buried deep enough. A small light at the end of the tunnel finally broke through my gloom. I decided to join the Carmelites. I entered the seminary the following fall. This proved to be one of the most significant decisions in my life. This was my invitation into "the Jesus game," where you often win by losing when it comes to prayer: "For whoever wishes to save his life will lose it, but whoever loses his life for my sake and the sake of the Gospel will save it" (Lk 14:35).

These two incidents help us see that prayer is not an easy topic to discern. When I was in fourth grade, we were in the midst of the Second World War, in which fifty million people lost their lives. I am sure we prayed for peace in our classroom, but I do not remember it. Likewise, at that time, my brother John, just four months out of Mt. Carmel High

School, was in very dangerous circumstances in the Pacific. It would seem God had different priorities than my excitement for Notre Dame. My life's journey would teach me that as our prayer matures, we have to get in touch with God's priorities.

With the perspective of time, the message of this prayer story is the growth from seeing prayer as magical to real prayer. There is a transition from myself as the center to the lifelong struggle to put God at the center. There always seems to be an encounter with the darkness of confusion and pain that slowly opens up to light as we mature in prayer.

As we move forward to try to delve into the complexity of the prayer of petition, we would do well to first consider how our culture is a major hindrance to all kinds of prayer.

Our Culture as an Obstacle to Prayer
As a newly arrived and poorly informed immigrant in the exploding world of social media, I am going to use a more comfortable source, the evening news, as a vehicle for looking into our culture and the prayer of petition. There are two points I want to make. First of all, the evening news portrays prayer as shallow and truly inconsequential. Second, the evening news portrays success in our society quite forcefully. Prayer has a minimal role in this obvious and powerful lesson.

When the news encounters true experiences of our mortality, there never is any depth in the coverage. The mass shootings, the gang violence, the ravaging fires, the hurricanes and tornadoes all fall into a shallow ritual of coverage. The deeper issues are not addressed. There is never any sense that we are being exposed to the mystery of good and evil that clearly points out our mutual mortality.

The sense of prayer is almost always in some memorial of flowers and candles with the names of the victims. The survivors are presented in their anguish but very seldom in the true reality of their coming face to face with the deepest human reality, good and evil. They never address death as an integral part of life. Most often, there seems to be a rush to get to the weather and sports.

On a second level, the evening news carries a message of success. This dimension of the news is a much more powerful impediment to prayer. This norm of success pervades the news, the programs, and especially the advertising. True success involves the person who is in control, one who is able to acquire an endless amount of goods and products. The successful person achieves their goal. They amass an ever-expanding condition of independence. This relentless proclamation seeks to drive away any sense of morality and human frailty. The good guys never lose and never die. True happiness is right around the corner with the next purchase, which will guarantee a happiness almost without end. Prayer has little consequence in this authoritative and constant call to the good life.

The gospel message presents a radical alternative to the consumer society's good life. Simplicity, openness, acceptance, humility, compassion, and boundaries of inclusion that do not seem to end are some of the evangelical values that stand in harsh contrast to the success story that dominates our culture.

Prayer of Petition and Spiritual Maturity

The promise to pray for someone is a serious responsibility. We are entering a mystery where we recognize our helplessness in the hands of an all-loving and merciful God. Too often, our promise to pray is a shallow commitment. Much more often than not, the depth of our relationship to the person or situation we are addressing in our prayer determines the intensity and consistency of our prayer. The closer they are to us, the more authentic the prayer. The gospel is always about expanding the horizons of our concern. This is especially relevant in the object of our prayer.

God is patient with us. God's presence in life has a way of drawing us into a developing relationship with God. As our awareness of God grows, so too does the awareness of our self. Both our sinfulness and God's mercy slowly surface in our consciousness as we mature spiritually. This, in turn, enlightens us to the seriousness of prayer in contrast to our frequently casual approach to it. Prayer is a serious venture. It demands a committed faith. It requires a serious personal concern on our part to avoid making it trivial. The foundation of our prayer of petition to an all-knowing and all-loving God starts out with these prerequisites:

1. We are sinful and need to be aware that all healing and freedom flow from God's mercy.

2. All prayer begins with God's initiative.

3. Our request, whether spiritual or material, worldly or heavenly, must be in accord with God's plan, the Kingdom proclaimed by Jesus.

4. We must come to prayer in loving and trusting submission as creature to a compassionate Creator.

5. We must seek the attitude of Jesus in his final prayer: "Father, if you are willing, take this cup away from me; still, not my will but yours be done" (Lk 22:42).

These five insights lead to a prayer that is rooted in faith and nurtured by hope and love. As we grow in our awareness of God and of ourselves—true spiritual maturity—a fundamental insight slowly rises to the surface. Whatever we ask for in our prayer of petition must find its true meaning as part of God's overall plan of salvation. Our petitions have to fit into God's design, which is based on love and mercy without limit. God's providence is well beyond the confines of our human comprehension. This is why even the simplest of petitions in our prayer is rooted in the sacred and transcendent. Prayer is a serious activity.

These five elements help our prayer make sense in light of

an all-knowing and all-loving God. Ultimately, all true prayer has to fit into God's plans, and then, into our plans. In this context, we can begin to address the mystery of our suffering and loss in our unanswered petitions for very good things such as health, security, reconciliation, freedom from addiction, and so many others. Here we find ourselves in the great mystery of life: suffering and death and a continual experience of all the consequences of the original sin. This is the stuff of the crisis of the emergency room, the disturbing news in the doctor's office, and the meeting in the funeral parlor, where the limits of our broken human condition are raw and naked. Death is not only a remote possibility; it is staring us in the face. These are the circumstances where the magical god of our superficial wants and wishes gives way to the God revealed in the crucified and risen Christ. When our prayer of petition is not rooted in faith in this God, our prayer gradually slips more toward the magical. This gradual shift, which leads us to put ourselves at the center, will come up empty when the inevitable reality of our mortality rises to the fore.

It is also critical to remember that we come to God in prayer as we are: broken and sinful. We do not need to be saints or theologians to pray. God has a way of connecting to our sincerity no matter how simple or confused it may be. Pope Francis has this insight on God's availability to our prayer: "God does not hide himself from those who seek him with a sincere heart, even though they do so tentatively, and in a vague and haphazard manner" (*The Joy of the Gospel*, 71). The only way we can pray is from the concrete and historical situation that is our daily experience. True prayer, emerging from our bewilderment and ignorance, is a simple and beautiful expression of our dependence on God. We are recognizing our limits. We are standing face to face with the deepest truth of our being: a humble sinner accepted and loved by a gracious God. It truly does not matter if our prayer is answered in our terms. More important is a deeper truth: God is God and we are the sinful creature both loved and forgiven. In our prayer, we come to know ourselves as truly in the need of God's mercy and providential care.

In the next section I am going to delve into both the complexity and beauty of the prayer of petition. Then, in section three, I will present the Lord's Prayer, the Our Father, as the most fitting model of the prayer of petition.

FOR PRAYERFUL REFLECTION AND DISCUSSION

1. *Why is saying, "I will pray for you" taking on a serious responsibility? How might we put our prayer into action?*

2. *What is the difference between a magical approach to prayer and a mature approach to prayer?*

3. *What is the most challenging of the five elements of prayer of petition? What is the most freeing?*

11

Prayer of Petition Is Complex and Easily Distorted

I would like to share two very different incidents that expose some important aspects of this problem. When I was young, I always made the sign of the cross when I was at bat while playing baseball. There was an older agnostic neighbor who found great joy mocking me every time I made an out. His constant agitation drove me to become both angry and determined: I was Catholic and I was not going to change. My sign of the cross became less rooted in prayer, if it ever was, but rather an expression of a strong-minded anger and hostility. It became an obstacle on my journey to God. As simple as it was, the same type of provoking response had led to the religious wars over the centuries.

A second incident was much more serious. In a neighboring parish, a single mother lost her teenage son in a horrific accident. At the Mass of the Resurrection, one of the resident characters in the parish made an ugly scene. He stood next to the coffin berating the people that their failure to pray with deeper faith was the reason God was not raising this young man to life. The mother went to him and gently told him she had faith and trusted in God's will. She took him to his seat in a gesture of kindness and compassion.

Both of these incidents show how Christian prayer is always being pulled by selfishness and neglect of God. There are two fundamental points about the prayer of petition. We start with an awareness of our dependence on God. Second, whatever our petition may be, it must lead to God's plan for our salvation, the Kingdom proclaimed by Jesus in the gospels. As we slip away from these fundamental points, we move gradually into deeper levels of superstition and magic. This is a denial of God and a gross distortion of our faith. It is amazing how flawed Christian prayer fades into the same structure of petition as practiced in witchcraft.

The Church's prayer for a blessing of a car gives an important insight into this complex issue of the integrity of prayer of petition. The prayer of blessing makes three points: safety of those in the vehicle, the responsibility of the driver for the safety of others, and that Christ always be a companion of those in the vehicle.

This call for personal responsibility and accountability is critical to all prayer. God expects us to use the talents and gifts we have received. This task of human effort is spelled out beautifully in what we call the transcendental precepts. We express this human effort in the following guidelines for all authentic human activity:

1. Be attentive.
2. Be intelligent.
3. Be reasonable.
4. Be responsible.
5. Be loving.

In this way, whether in driving a car or any other genuine human activity, we are using our humanity as God wants. Only after this engagement should we enter the arena of the prayer of petition. By following the precepts, we develop a proper image of God. This is the loving providential God who operates within the limits of our sinful and broken human condition. God's saving plan was made manifest in the death and resurrection of Jesus. God invites us to share in that great act of love by our service and surrender.

This is our final and complete entry into God's loving plan. Along the way, everything we pray for needs to be measured in how it helps us achieve this final good that is God's will for us.

When we move away from this journey of faith and trust, we move into the magical. We create our own image of God as our personal Divine Manipulator. In this context, we become the center, and God is there in heaven at our beck and call. Now, it is not God's Kingdom but our kingdom that is front and center. Most often our desires are for security and the elimination of anxiety. Usually our prayer falls into a pattern of seeking some form of prosperity usually defined not by God's Kingdom but by the norms of our consumer society with its assurance of wealth and comfort.

Jesus has much to say about prayer in the gospels. In Luke, Jesus makes it very clear how to decide about our concerns and God's concerns. "Therefore, I tell you, do not worry about your life and what you will eat, or about your body and what you will wear. For life is more than food and the body more than clothing. Notice the ravens: they do not sow or reap; they have neither storehouse nor barn, yet God feeds them. How much more important are you than birds!…Indeed, seek his kingdom, and these other things will be given you besides…for where your treasure is, there also will your heart be" (Lk 12:22–24, 31, 34).

In all of its complexity, the prayer of petition comes down to this. God is God. We are creatures. This is the basis of our relationship with God. As creatures we are ultimately defined by our mortality resulting from our sinfulness. Our basic petition is for freedom from this bondage. That is God's plan for us: a freedom and love in this life that opens in the passage through death to life eternal.

God's Plan and Our Plan
Most often, when people pray, their petition fits into *their* plan. They want God to respond when their strategy for happiness needs some help. But God also has a plan, and God wants us to respond to the divine plan. Here is the conflict, the two plans: God's and ours. This is a significant problem with prayer. However, in the end, this difference can be a great source of life in our prayer.

I had my first experience of the conflict of the two plans in high school. The loss of a championship football game seemed like the end of the world to me. In fact, it was the beginning of a new and ever-so-more-wonderful world. After the loss of the game, I entered what seemed like an unending funk totally new to my teenage experience. What it was in reality was God making space so I could hear his call to enter the seminary, one of the best decisions in my life. It took me many years to understand that the pain and anguish of the loss were a true blessing. Life is always coming from death when we walk with Jesus.

For most people, a good part of their journey as Christians and searching people involves this transition from our plan for happiness to God's plan for our happiness. We are clear with what we want and what we think we need. It is like the adult list for Santa. However, through the experience of life's many trials, we gradually see the need to ease off of our agenda and "*let go.*" Then we gradually come to see and embrace the need to "*let God!*" This maturation is one of the important functions on the Christian journey.

FOR PRAYERFUL REFLECTION AND DISCUSSION

1. *What are the two fundamental points about prayer of petition in this chapter? Do you agree with them?*

2. *What is our role when we pray? What is God's role?*

3. *How might we align our prayers of petition with God's call for us?*

III

The Deepest Expression of Prayer

The Our Father

Our reflection on the prayer of petition leads quite naturally to the Our Father, the Lord's Prayer. It is the culmination and deepest expression of all the prayers in the Bible. It has been described as the summary of the gospel.

Down through the centuries, the saints, and particularly the Doctors of the Church, have sung its praises. St. Augustine wrote seven different commentaries on this prayer. He declared it contains all we have to say in our prayer. St. John of the Cross said the seven petitions express all our needs, both temporal and spiritual. St. Thomas Aquinas called it a prayer of the end times. At our present moment we experience the mystery of salvation in what has been described as *"already but not yet."* This means that the paschal mystery of Christ's death and resurrection has accomplished our salvation. Yet we are in a process of moving toward the completion of that reality in our Christian life and the final destiny of human history. We are moving toward the fullness of the Kingdom of God, the restoration of the original innocence. It still remains an object of hope, a time when we will be completely free of the consequences of sin: no more sickness, division, hatred, violence, ignorance, dehumanizing poverty and prejudice, and, finally, death giving way to eternal life. St. Thomas's point is that the Our Father is a prayer for the coming of the New Day and the New Creation that is God's Kingdom.

In our day, the Our Father seems to fall far short of such grandeur. It appears much more mundane. We fail to grasp much of its depth connected to our salvation history as well as its crucial role in all of the Church's prayer. I would venture to say that the Hail Mary is more often the choice when most people are driven to the prayer of petition by an immediate personal crisis.

We need a deeper understanding and, in particular, a more

prayerful experience of this treasure of our faith. It guides our desire for the right things in accord with God's will for us. This prayer of Jesus is not directed to win over God with many words. Its goal is to prepare the human heart to receive God's generosity in the completion of this saving action in our daily life.

After the initial address, the prayer has seven petitions. The focus of the "thou petitions" is on God and an authentic recognition of God's worthiness and dominion. They seek true appreciation of God's holiness, the New Day of the Kingdom, and that the will of God be done at all times. These first three petitions are totally interconnected. In fact, the first and third, holiness and God's will, are included in the dominating truth of the Kingdom. The coming of the Kingdom, the central message of Jesus, is the beginning of the destruction of the evil forces that have enslaved the world.

The final four are the "we petitions." In these requests we appeal for our basic human needs. They are the foundation of what we require to fulfill our loving response to God stated in the "thou petitions." In this list of our needs, there also is a sense of the future. We are moving toward that moment of completion that is the fullness of God's holiness and will in the Kingdom. Our fundamental reality is set before us: God is Creator, loving and merciful, and we are the creatures, mortal and sinful. Yet we are loved and forgiven and called to the pilgrimage of the New Day of the Kingdom.

The Thou Petitions

Our

When we say "*Our*" at the beginning and "*us*" in our final petitions, we are stating a reality. We are involved with all others. This calls us beyond our personal concerns. We are invited into the constant gospel message of inclusion in opposition to exclusion. Our love is in a constant process of expansion. The term "Our" identifies us as part of the family of God. Jesus is creating a community of believers to share his relationship with the Father. All our prayers include personal needs but also take account of all God's children. All the petitions in this prayer are communal as well as personal.

One example of this social dimension of our prayer is concern for the hungry of the world. "Our" daily bread is just that, bread for all. The parables of Lazarus and Matthew 25 are two of many specific gospel expressions of this concern for our neighbor.

Father/Abba

In the Old Testament, there are only fourteen references to God as father. These passages in the Hebrew Scriptures never imply the concept of God as procreator or ancestor as found in the Gentile religions. The term Father always refers to the one who elected, delivered, and saved his people Israel by mighty deeds in history.

In teaching the disciples to pray, however, Jesus uses the term Abba, the intimate expression of an adult child for their father. This establishes the context for the prayer.

In the term Abba, the ultimate mystery of Christ's mission and authority is unveiled. Having grown into the deep knowledge of God, Jesus addresses him as Abba and, more amazingly, taught his followers to do the same. He gives them a share of his sonship and empowers them as his disciples to speak with their Father in such a familiar and trusting way. Jesus is creating a community of disciples that will be a "family of God." Jesus wants his followers to enter into a relationship of intimacy and trust just like his with the Father. We are invited to enter more deeply into the great mystery that Jesus presents when he invites us to pray to our father.

There is a point of caution one must make. Each of us personally, and all in our different cultures, has a distinct experience of our parents. There is a great variety, both good and bad. Jesus says, "No one knows the Son except the Father and no one knows the Father except the Son and anyone to whom the Son chooses to reveal him" (Mt 11:27). We are in need of great humility in forming our image and relationship with God as Abba. It transcends all human limitations. All of Jesus' teachings call us to both a sense of incredible intimacy and of the total "otherness" of God. The Christian life is a journey of purification of this relationship with God as Abba. The Catholic Catechism has a series of phrases that describe the depth and beauty of intimacy we are called to when we address God as Abba: straightforward simplicity, filial trust, joyous assurance, humble boldness, and the certainty of being loved.

Who Art in Heaven

In the prayer, "heaven" is one of many words that we must understand more deeply to truly enter the mystery of this great prayer. Heaven does not refer to a place. Our gracious God transcends space. This heaven is our true homeland toward which we are heading and to which we already belong. It means the majesty of God in the hearts of the faithful. We are not addressing a faraway God but one within our hearts. The journey is within to our true home.

Hallowed Be Thy Name

Hallowed means to make holy. The request here is that we recognize God's holiness and respond to that divine holiness in our lives. We are witnesses to God's holiness as we follow in the footsteps of Jesus in search of his Kingdom.

Thy Kingdom Come

The assumption of all salvation history, the story of the Bible, is the loss of innocence as a result of the sin of our first parents, Adam and Eve. The world has been in the hands of the forces of evil ever since. Humankind is in bondage to sin and death. All are alienated from the true source of life. God's plan of salvation is the reversal of these forces of evil, the restoration of innocence.

Throughout the whole Old Testament there is a growing sense of Promise, the sense of God's coming. There is a mounting hope of deliverance. All these forces of good are integrated in the fundamental message of Jesus: "This is the time of fulfillment. The kingdom of God is at hand. Repent and believe in the gospel" (Mk 1:15). This is the call to freedom, the call to integrity and wholeness. The Kingdom captures every human aspiration that we have to be free, to celebrate life, for a world of justice and peace and the integrity of creation and deliverance from sin and death. We pray for that new day, when sickness will give way to well-being, when blindness of body and spirit will be consumed in light, when ignorance will be shattered by truth.

The Kingdom of love and mercy, of justice and peace, is already here in Christ's victory over death. Yet Christ's transformation of individuals, societies, and cultures is happening only slowly as the human venture moves toward its conclusion as the gospel is proclaimed to all. This is truly the "already but not yet" of God's saving actions. The Kingdom is Jesus and all he means to us in his gospel message.

When we pray as Jesus taught us to plead for the Kingdom, we are permeated with a sense of hope. We begin to comprehend the power of sin and death in our day. We see this in the inequity of the distribution of wealth, the depth of racism and sexism, the utter waste of wars and violence in our midst, flowing from irrational use of guns and the absolute neglect of our environment leading to the dire consequences of climate change. We need to turn to Jesus and pray for the coming of the Kingdom. In the end, only God will deliver us from the depth of the brokenness and destruction that we face.

The Kingdom is God's gift but part of that gift is our responsibility to work for its completion. We must acknowledge our weakness. God is the Creator and we are the creatures. Yet our life has consequences. We are accountable. This is what it means to "repent and believe in the gospel." When we get in touch with the giftedness of the Kingdom, when we accept the mystery of God's hidden presence and action in our daily life, we begin to understand Paul's words: "When I am weak, then I am strong" (2 Cor 9:10). God uses our weakness.

The Kingdom, the restoration of innocence, has already come with the saving acts of Jesus' death and resurrection. We are now in the final days awaiting the conclusion of that saving history. We live amidst the weeds and the wheat where the separation will only come at the end at God's harvest time. We are passing inevitably to the day of complete victory where prejudice, isolation, and exclusion will gradually but absolutely give way to acceptance, reconciliation, and inclusion. Peace will hold dominion. We will eventually see the fullness of God's power wipe away every tear, and swords will be transformed into plowshares. Hospitals and cemeteries will be the stuff of yesteryear. The sting of death will be totally crippled in the final victory of the Lamb! This will be the triumph of God's promise in the Kingdom.

Love, justice, and mercy have the final say in the Kingdom. Our sins are forgiven, the sick healed, enemies are reconciled, the poor share the blessings of the Lord in abundance, and the captives are freed. Every desire in harmony with God's love is fulfilled. The human venture is brought to a just and peaceful resolution.

Thy Will Be Done on Earth as It Is in Heaven

Jesus showed us the way in fulfilling the Father's will. God's will draws us into the truth and the fullness of salvation. God's plan is for our freedom leading to eternal happiness. God invites us into that treasure beyond our dreams. In Gethsemane, Jesus showed the power of his surrender to the Father's will. His acceptance of the divine will was the passage from death to life for all humankind. God's will for us, both personally and communally, continues to call us into the fullness of life.

The We Petitions

Give Us This Day Our Daily Bread
By saying give "us" we are showing our communion with all our brothers and sisters. The bread we ask for includes all material needs of ourselves and others. As part of a communion, the needs of others, especially the poor, must be a priority.

At the same time, we are praying for the Bread of Life, which includes the word of God and the Body of Christ in the Eucharist. These gifts of the Spirit strengthen us and enable us to respond generously to the thou petitions.

Forgive Us Our Trespasses as We Forgive Those Who Trespass against Us
Reconciliation looks forward to the coming of the Lord in judgment. We are asking for the great gift necessary to enter the Kingdom: forgiveness. Only our willingness to forgive will open the passage to new life. Lack of forgiveness hardens our hearts and closes the way into the merciful love of our God.

And Lead Us Not into Temptation
We now recognize our human weakness caught in the battle of the spirit and the flesh. We are asking God to protect and guide us away from sin. We are asking for discernment, vigilance, and perseverance.

But Deliver Us from Evil

This really means to deliver us from the Evil One, who is Satan. We are asking for guidance through the harsh and horrible appeal of all elements in the world that are in total opposition to our salvation. We are asking God to deliver us from all the evils that are the relentless work of the Evil One whose overriding desire is to draw us away from God.

FOR PRAYERFUL REFLECTION AND DISCUSSION

1. *How is the Our Father the "deepest expression of prayer"?*

2. *Why do we begin this prayer with, "Our Father" rather than, "My Father"?*

3. *How might we infuse the Lord's Prayer with more meaning at Mass and in our personal prayer practice?*

CONCLUSION

When I was a young priest, an old, wise pastor gave me some great advice. He said, "Tracy, keep your eye on the ball. The priest's job is quite simple. We deal with the great ultimate issues of life, love, and death. Everything else needs to give way to these deep realities." I have come to truly appreciate the wisdom of my mentor's insight. Likewise, I see the prayer of petition growing in this direction. Everything in life that is truly important is rooted in the great themes of life, love, and death. If we have these basic elements in order, God is at the center of our lives. Our maturing process helps us to slowly discern what is truly important in this area. We become able to identify those things that fit the "cotton candy stuff of life," those things and experiences that look so good but quickly evaporate into nothing.

Our prayer should be moving us to respond to the deep and wise themes of life, love, and death. We will connect our experience to the presence of God as we slowly see what is truly important on our journey. As we grow in maturity and wisdom, the more clearly we will move our priorities from things to people, from possessions to relationships, from fear to trust. Life, love, and death are the passageway to God. Attention to these themes will draw us into the Kingdom that Jesus proclaimed.

Jesus taught us to pray for the great things: for God's glory and Kingdom, and that God's great gifts—the bread of life and his endless mercy—may be granted even here, now, today. Through these great gifts, God will more than take care of the ordinary cares and worries of daily life that so often occupy the center of our prayer life. As we grow in our understanding and acceptance of this overwhelming truth of the gospel, we will see that the Kingdom holds the answer to all our prayers and to the themes of life, love, and death. "So do not worry and say, 'what are we to eat?' or 'What are we to drink?' or 'What are we to wear?' All these things the pagans seek. Your heavenly Father knows that you need them all. But seek first the kingdom of God and his righteousness, and all these things will be given you besides" (Mt 6:31–33).